LEARN ABOUT
GERMANY
For Kids

This Book Belongs to:

_____

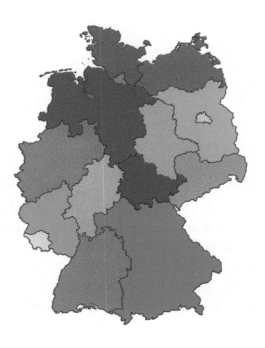

Flossis in Düsseldorf, Germany

Learn About Germany Contents

Learn About Germany Contents

Where is Germany?

North Sea

Denmark

Baltic Sea

Netherlands

Belgium

Luxembourg

Germany

Poland

Czech Republic

France

Austria

Switzerland

Germany shares borders with nine other countries!

To make it easier for residents and visitors of neighbouring countries to travel without customs and border control, the **Schengen Area** was created in 1995. At first, only Germany, Belgium, Luxembourg, the Netherlands and France belonged to the Schengen Area. But today, **27** European countries have signed the agreement. This means that once you arrive in Germany, you can travel to another Schengen country without showing your passport.

Germany Has Sixteen States

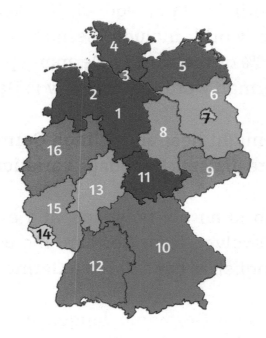

1. Niedersachsenn - Lower Saxony
2. Bremen
3. Hamburg
4. Schleswig-Holstein
5. Mecklenburg-Vorpommern
6. Brandenburg
7. Berlin
8. Sachsen-Anhalt (Saxony-Anhalt)
9. Sachsen (Saxony)
10. Bayern (Bavaria)
11. Thüringen (Thuringia)
12. Baden-Württemberg
13. Hessen
14. Saarland
15. Rheinland-Pfalz (Rhindland-Palatinate)
16. Nordrhein-Westfalen (North Rhine-Westphalia)

The Language

German is the official language of Germany. Only six countries in the world include German as an official language. Over 78% of the world's German speakers live in Germany. The German word for Germany is Deutschland.

In Germany, you might hear about "high German" and "low German"; these are dialects (language variations).

Fun Fact: German is an old language, and as of today, 47 other languages evolved from German. Including English! So technically, English is considered a Germanic language.

Because English is a Germanic language, sentences are structured in the same way (syntax and grammar). English and German place adjectives and adverbs before nouns, for example, "the red car". But the noun comes first in Romance languages (like French and Spanish). In this example, a Spaniard would say, "El auto rojo" (the car red). For this reason, English speakers might find German easier to learn than Spanish because the sentence structure makes sense to us.

Sprichst du Deutsch?

Do you speak German?

Polite German Words to Learn

Please - bitte (**bit**-tuh)
Thank you - danke (**dunk**-eh)
Thank you very much - danke schön (**dunk**-eh shune)

Although bitte means "please", it is also a way to say "you're welcome". If someone says "danke", you can respond with "bitte". If someone says "danke schön", you can respond with "bitte schön".

Excuse me - verzeihung (fer-**tsai**-ung)
Hello - hallo (**ha**-lo)
How Are You? - Wie geht's dir? (vee-gets-diar)
Good, thank you - gut, danke (goot, **dunk**-eh)

I am called (or my name is) - ich heiße (isch hi-ssehr)

Hallo, ich heiße Julien

ß makes the double-s sound

Funny German Idioms

An idiom is a phrase that makes no sense when translated but is used as a common expression. For example, in English, we use the idiom "once in a blue moon" to mean it happens rarely. Here are some funny German idioms:

Hätte, hätte, fahrradkette
translation - would have, would have, bike chain
meaning - I wish I could have done it differently

Schlafen bis die puppen
translation - sleep until the dolls
meaning - sleep for a long time

Ich gehe um die ecke
translation - I'm going around the corner
meaning - I'm going to the bathroom

Da war tote hose
translation - there was dead pants
meaning - the gathering was boring

Money in Germany

The currency in Germany is the euro. Germany was one of the first countries to adopt the euro in 1999. Today, twenty European countries use the euro.

The euro's value can change throughout the year depending on complicated factors. But as of the writing of this book in 2023, one euro is equal to:

1.09 American dollars ($)
1.47 Canadian dollars ($)
0.88 British pounds (£)

The symbol for the euro looks like this:

The German Flag

The German flag is a basic tri-colour flag with black, red and gold. Like most countries, the flag changes through history. This current flag has been official since 1949. Although the flag is young, the three colours were established as Germany's official colours in the mid-1800s.

Belgium Flag

Germany's flag looks a lot like Belgium's flag, except the stripes are laid out differently.

The Weather in Germany

The mountainous central and southern regions can affect Germany's weather, so within 100 kilometres, you can notice a significant change in the climate. However, in general, Germany enjoys all four seasons.

Although the winter is cold and they have snow, it is warmer in Germany than in Canada or the northern American states. The coldest month is January, and the temperatures average -2°C to 6°C (29°F - 43°F)*.

The hottest month is July. Temperatures range from an average of 15°C to 27°C (58°F - 80°F).

If the weather is important, then the best time to visit Germany is between May to September. But this is all just a matter of opinion. October and December are also popular times to visit Germany for reasons other than weather.

*C is for Celsius, the measurement used in Canada and the United Kingdom, and F is for Fahrenheit in the United States.

Some Reasons to Visit Germany in the Fall & Winter

Octoberfest

See Page 37

See Page 39

Christmas Market

Fasching Fastnacht Karneval

See Page 38

The Population of Germany

As of April 2023, the population of Germany was about 84,522,000 people.

Germany has three cities with a population of more than a million people:

Berlin: 3,426,354
Hamburg 1,739,117
Munich 1,260,391

Population Density

Population density is the number of people living within one square kilometre (km), dividing a country's population by the total land area. Let's compare countries:

Country	Population Density per sq. km.
United States	37
United Kingdom	279
Bangladesh	1,315
Denmark	147
Australia	3
Taiwan	660
Germany	239
Italy	200
France	118
Spain	95
Mexico	66
Singapore	8,323
Iceland	3
Canada	4

As you can see, Germany has a population density of 239 people per square kilometre.

Is your country on the list? Is Germany more crowded or less crowded than your country?

What Kind of Homes do Germans Live in?

More than half of Germany's population lives in a rental accommodation. This is the highest percentage in all of Europe. This is because the house prices and required deposits are very high, making it difficult to afford your own house.

In recent years, Germans have become more creative with their housing. For example, houseboats, motorhomes and tiny houses are becoming more popular. Plus they're really cool!

Schools in Germany

In Germany, homeschooling is illegal, with just a few exceptions. About 1,000 children are being homeschooled in Germany, either severely ill, the children of diplomats, or child actors. Those are the only exceptions. Otherwise, all children between six and fifteen must attend school.

Fun Fact: Most children attend kindergarten for three years! Kindergarten is not mandatory, but it is free. Kids can attend from ages three to six, and it goes for a half day.

Fun Fact: Children in Germany don't eat lunch at school. They have a long morning break for a snack; then they are usually finished the school day by 1:30 when they go home to have lunch and do their homework. There is one exception: a gesamtschule (see page 16).

Primary and Secondary Schools

Every child in Germany aged six and older must attend school. Schools are free, but there are private and international schools that can charge tuition.

Most primary schools (grundschule) finish after grade four (except in Berlin and Brandenburg, where they attend until grade six). Once the child completes primary school, the teacher recommends which of three types of secondary school (weiterführende schule) they should attend based on their performance in primary school. This is called streaming. The three secondary schools are called hauptschule, realschule and gymnasium.

Hauptschule goes from grades five to nine for children likely to enter the trades. Hauptschule graduates can move on to a trade school but do not qualify to enter university. Realschule continues to grade 10. After that, the student can move to a gymnasium if their grades are good. Gymnasium goes to grade 12 or 13 and prepares the students for university. Although the primary school teacher makes the recommendations, the parents get the final say regarding which secondary school their child will attend.

Finally, once a child is ready for secondary school, they may decide not to enter one of the three tracks mentioned above and instead attend a gesamtschule to grade 13. This is a combination of the three, with one big difference: a gesamtschule goes for longer days and is the only type of school with a lunch cafeteria.

Popular Schoolyard Games

Schoolyard games in Germany are similar to other places in the world. The most popular and familiar games are:

- Eins, Zwei, Drei...Halt! (1, 2, 3...stop! or red light/green light)
- Gummitwist (elastics or jump rope)
- Hupfspiel (hopscotch)
- Fangen (tag)
- Dosenfussball (kick the can)

Popular Schoolyard Games
Sardinen (Hiding Sardines)

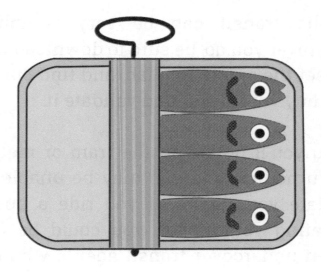

This game is much like hide-and-seek, except it's played with three or more players (the more players, the better). It's also a game meant for a large outdoor area like a park or schoolyard, but be sure to set boundaries for the game.

The person who is "it" hides while the other kids close their eyes and count to a previously agreed-upon number. Once the number is reached, they all look for the hider. Once found, the finder quietly hides alongside the hider. Each time players find the hiders, they quietly hide with them.

When only one player is left, that person is "it" and becomes the hider for the next game.

Can you guess why the game is called Hiding Sardines?

Public Transit in Germany
Tips to Share With Your Parents

Regional public transit can be very complicated in Germany. Wherever you go, be sure to download the transit app. You can set the app to English, and find out what you need to know, buy your ticket and validate it.

The first thing you'll notice on the tram or metro is that there are no turnstiles, and you may be unable to find a place to validate your ticket. If you ride a bus or train without validating your ticket, you could be fined €60. There are often undercover transit agents who could ask you for proof.

Although public transit in Germany is clean, modern and safe, the ticket system can be complicated and confusing for tourists. There will always be an information desk at the train or bus station; they are very helpful (and speak English).

Two more tips: for national travel across Germany, try to buy your train ticket as far in advance as possible (you can purchase it up to 90 days before your trip). The price becomes much more expensive the closer to the travel date. A train ticket from one major city to another could cost more than a plane ticket! Also, pay the extra fee to reserve your seats. Otherwise, you may have to stand for hours.

Berlin Train Station

ICE Train in Frankfurt

The Autobahn

Germany is famous for its autobahn, a series of highways throughout the country where the speed limit is just a suggestion. Here are some fun facts about the autobahn: If your parents rent a car in Germany, be sure to show this to them.

- Your vehicle must travel at least 60 km/h (37.3 mph), so scooters are not allowed.
- There are no tolls or billboards.
- With 13,192 kilometres (8,197 miles), the autobahn is the fourth largest highway network in the world.
- Road signs do not use cardinal directions (north, south, east, west). Instead, directions point to the nearest cities.
- You'll see many signs that say "ausfahrt", which means "exit."
- If a police car wants to pull you over, instead of coming up behind you, they will pull in front of you, and a sign will light up that says "bitter folgen," which means "please follow". You must follow the police car, and they will take you to where it is safe to stop.
- The recommended speed on the autobahn is 130 km (about 80 mph) - this is not enforced.
- The highest recorded speed on the autobahn is 423 km (263 mph).
- Statistically, Germany has the same number of fatal car accidents as the rest of Europe, proving the autobahn is no more dangerous than other highways.
- Trucks are not allowed on the autobahn on Sundays or holidays.

Renting a Bike in Germany

Fun Fact: Of all the countries in the world, Germany is the most bike-friendly overall.

In a 2022 study*, Germany made the top ten bike-friendly countries list three times!

Munster ranked #2
Breman ranked #9
Hanover ranked #10

- Source: Euronews.next, 28/12/2022

A great way to explore Germany is by bike. There are several bike rental companies; one of the biggest rental companies is located in 60 German cities and is done through an app on your phone. One app can be used for a family of up to four people.

But before you rent a bike, you have to understand some important rules:

- Unless there is a sign to say otherwise, only kids can ride a bike on the sidewalk. Adults must use the road or a bike lane.

- A bell and a light are required, but a helmet is not (but helmets are always recommended).

- You must ride with the traffic unless there is a sign on the road with a picture of a bike and the word "frei"; then, you can ride in any direction.

Where To Go in Germany

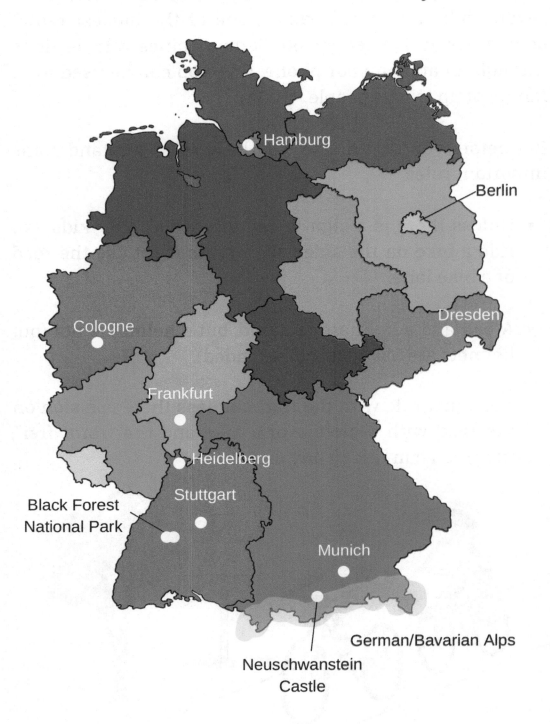

Berlin - The Capital of Germany

The **Brandenburg Gate** marks the entrance to the City of Berlin. It was built over 200 years ago and symbolises peace and freedom. Important events have occurred there, like speeches by famous leaders and concerts by famous musicians. People from all over the world come to see it and take pictures in front of it.

A wall once divided the country into East and West Germany. People on one side could not go to the other side, and families were separated. But in 1989, the wall finally came down. It was an event celebrated worldwide because tearing down the wall symbolised freedom. The **Berlin Wall Memorial** is where people can see parts of the old wall and learn more about what happened.

Berlin

The Museum Für Naturkunde (**Museum of Natural History**) is a fantastic place to see dinosaur bones and other artefacts from thousands of years ago. But this museum isn't just about the past; there are also exhibits related to science and the future.

If you prefer living animals, then the **Berlin Zoo** and Aquarium is there for you. It's one of the world's oldest and most famous zoos. The Berlin Zoo is home to the largest variety of species in the world and is the only place in Germany you can see giant pandas!

Berlin's Pink Pipes

If you travel to Berlin, one of the things you'll notice immediately are the pink pipes throughout the city.

The ground under Berlin is very marshy, and the huge amount of water can cause basement flooding and make construction difficult. So they needed a way to pump the water from the ground and into the river. Since they couldn't hide the pipes, they painted them pink and made them a fun part of the city's landscape. A psychologist recommended pink because it's often the favourite colour for children.

Why all the twists and turns in the pipes? It's because if the temperature is cold, the pipe might shrink and break. Adding the curves takes the stress off the pipes. Besides that, the curves add interest and makes the whole system look like an art installation (which is what many tourists think it is!).

Munich

Munich is Bavaria's capital and the original home to Germany's famous Oktoberfest (see page 37).

The City of Munich has more than a dozen museums that would appeal to children, including the Spielzeugmuseum (Toy Museum).

Eisbachwelle is one of Munich's top tourist attractions. Never thought people could surf in Munich? Well, they can! The family can enjoy a picnic and a day in the Englischer Garten (English Garden) and enjoy watching the professional surfers on this manufactured river. Unfortunately, the waves can be dangerous, so beginner surfers are not allowed. However, watching can be a lot of fun!

Neuschwanstein Castle

The building of this castle began in 1869 and was completed in 1880. It was commissioned by King Ludwig II, who lived there for only a few weeks. As the story goes, the banks threatened to seize the castle in 1885. The government declared King Ludwig II insane and forced him to leave. The King was found dead in a nearby river along with his psychiatrist, who had declared him insane. Was it a murder-suicide? No one knows for sure.

Today, the castle is owned by the Bavarian Palace Department and is one of the most visited castles in the world. It's a two-hour drive from Munich. You can tour the castle, but you are not allowed to take pictures inside.

Fun Fact: It is pronounced noy-**shvaan**-stine.

Alpsee Berwelt Sommerodelbahn

Does a summer toboggan run (sommerodelbahn) sound like fun? Well, it is! And Germany has several of them. One of the most popular, Alpsee Berwelt, is less than an hour's drive from Neuschwanstein Castle.

Although it's called a "summer" toboggan, at Alpsee, you can also ride in the winter. Take the ski lift up and the toboggan down.

Children aged three to eight can ride as a passenger, and children aged eight and older can ride alone. It might seem dangerous, but the cars have hand brakes if you get nervous.

If you love the thrill of a rollercoaster or a toboggan, check out one of Germany's sommerodelbahns!

The Black Forest

If you're a family of hikers and nature lovers, then The Black Forest should be on your list of places to visit. Besides dark pine forests, beautiful little villages and stunning waterfalls, you can also see the world's largest cuckoo clock!

The area covers about 3,734 km (2,320 miles) and is one of Germany's most popular tourist spots.

Fun Fact: Grimms Fairly Tales has its origins in The Black Forest.

Hamburg

Speicherstadt (warehouse city) is a UNESCO World Heritage Site* located in Hamburg. The building used to be a series of warehouses to store shipped goods. But today, Speicherstadt is a fun place to visit. You can see the world's largest model railway, take a spooky trip through an old dungeon, and visit a maritime and auto museum.

You can visit the zoo, aquarium or several museums in Hamburg. If you're there at the right time, you can also go to the funfair, held three times a year for a month.

Planten un Blomen is an urban park in Hamburg. The name Planten un Blomen is Low German (see page 3). It is also called "Pflanzen und Blumen" or "Plants and Flowers" in English. Whatever you call it, it's a beautiful park with pretty flowers and interesting plants.

- UNESCO stands for United Nations Educational, Scientific and Cultural Organization. A World Heritage Site means UNESCO deems it to have "outstanding universal value".

Cologne

Cologne has a lot of fun places to go if you're a kid. Like the zoo, aquarium, or even a chocolate factory where you can make your own chocolate bar!

If you are in Cologne from April through November, then be sure to visit the huge amusement park and water park. You'll need to drive about 45 minutes outside Cologne, but it's worth it.

The Cologne Cathedral is Germany's most visited landmark, the world's biggest twin-spired Church, and northern Europe's largest Gothic Church*.

*Gothic is a style of architecture from the 12th - 16th century.

Heidelberg

Fun Fact: Heidelberg is home to the oldest university in Germany (Heidelberg University), founded in 1386!

The most popular tourist destination and most famous landmark in Heidelberg is **Heidelberg Castle** (Schloss Heidelberg). The castle was built in 1214. But in 1537, lightning struck it, destroying the upper castle. Since that time, the castle has endured war and age. In 1900, it was finally decided not to restore the castle but preserve it as it is.

People enjoy touring the ruins for history but are also rewarded with a magnificent view of the city.

German Festivals

Germany is world famous for **Oktoberfest.** This festival is held all over Germany annually from mid-September to the first Sunday in October. The festival is an important part of Bavarian culture and has been running there since 1810.

Famous for its beer gardens, the festival is known for rides, games and food. Octoberfest (English spelling) is celebrated in countries all over the world, but Munich Germany is the OG (original).

Fun Fact: Oktoberfest is visited by more than six million people yearly.

Fasching, Fastnacht, Karneval

This is a huge pre-Lent celebration in Germany, but the name can be confusing. In northern Germany, they call it Fastnacht or Karneval. But in Bavaria, it's called Fasching.

The carnival season begins in mid-November and until February, when it ends with a big parade. Kids love to get dressed up, and department stores always make room for costumes for this time of year.

Christmas Markets

No one knows how to put together a Christmas Market better than the Germans. Whether you are in a tiny remote village or the centre of a major city, a fairy-tale-like Christmas market (Christkindlmarkt) will be nearby until the end of November and right through to just before Christmas Eve.

You can expect traditional handicrafts, handmade toys, ornaments, local food, culture, and entertainment. Germany has no "best" Christmas Market because they are all very special. The oldest market is the Dresdner Striezelmarkt in Dresden. It has over 230 booths and is the world's largest nutcracker.

German Food

Sausages (würste). This is a huge category of food in Germany. Most common is bratwurst.

Königsberger Klopse (boiled meatballs) are made with veal, onions, eggs, anchovies and spices, and is served with a creamy white sauce with capers.

Maultaschen are like ravioli except bigger. It's made with minced meat, breadcrumbs, onions and spinach. You can find these all over Germany, even frozen in the grocery stores.

German Food

Currywurst is a popular street food. The sausages are served with a mixture of ketchup and curry powder.

Schnitzel. Both Austria and Italy take credit for schnitzel, but they make it with veal. German schnitzel however, is made with pork or turkey.

Käsespätzle is a sort of pasta baked with cheese and decorated with fried onions. It's a popular dish at beer gardens and pubs.

German Desserts

Apfelstrudel (Apple Strudel) is the most popular pastry in Germany. It's baked apples wrapped in pastry and topped with whipped cream.

Schwarzwälder Kirschtorte (Black Forest Cake) is basically chocolate sponge cake, layered with cherry filling and whipped cream.

Spaghettieis is a fun dessert meant to look like a plate of spagetti. It's acutally gelato ice cream that was run through a pasta press, topped with strawberry sauce and sprinkled with white chocolate.

Wild Animals Found in Germany

Wild Boar

Badger

Deer

Wild Animals Found in Germany

Chamois

Beaver
(endangered)

Wolf - became
extinct in
Germany in
1904, but were
reintroduced
and the
population is
growing

Wild Animals Found in Germany

Raccoon (introduced from North America in the 20th century)

Red Fox

Alpine Marmot

Wild Birds Found in Germany

Golden Eagle

Long Eared Owl

Common Buzzard

Famous German Inventions

Helicopter

Diesel Engine

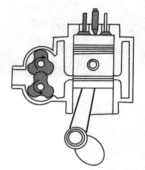

Harmonica

Accordian

Aspirin

Bunsen Burner

Contact Lenses

Famous German Inventions

Refrigerator

Bicycle

Beer

Chip Card

Gummi Bear

Tape

Airbag

A Brief History of Germany

Early Germany

The country was made up of small states ruled by kings and dukes.

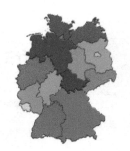

1871

Politician Otto von Bismarck brought the states together to become one country.

1914

World War I - Germany and its allies lost the war to Britain, France, the US and their allies.

1933

Adolf Hitler and the Nazi Party came to power.

1939

Hitler invaded Poland, starting World War II.

1945

World War II ends and Hitler dies.

1949

Germany formally split into two independent nations: West Germany, allied with Western democracies, and East Germany, allied with the Soviet Union. This started the Cold War.

A Brief History of Germany

1961

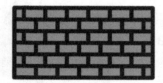

East German soldiers laid down more than 30 miles of barbed wire through the centre of Berlin. East Berlin citizens were forbidden to pass into West Berlin. This later became the Berlin Wall.

1989

The Cold War ended, and the Berlin Wall was torn down, causing celebrations worldwide.

2002

German currency changed from the Deutsche Mark to the Euro.

2023

Germany shuts down the last of their nuclear power stations as they transition to renewable energy.

Fun Facts

- Germans are the second largest beer consumers in the world (the Irish are number one).

- The first printed book was in German.

- Most German taxis are Mercedes-Benz.

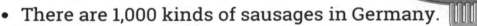

- There are 1,000 kinds of sausages in Germany.

- German words tend to be long. The longest word in the German dictionary is 79 letters long! The word is **rinderkennzeichnungsfleischetikettierung-süberwachungsaufgabenübertragungsgesetz** and it means delegation transfer law for cattle labelling and beef labelling supervision duties.

Fun Facts

- The first Oktoberfest was Prince Ludwig's wedding.

- The tradition of a Christmas tree (tannenbaum) began in Germany.

- Berlin is nine times bigger than Paris and has the largest train station in Europe.

- German is the fifth most widely taught language in the world.

- Germany has a nickname: Das Land der Dichter und Denker (Land of Poets and Thinkers).

Traditions in Germany

Father's Day in Germany has a strange tradition. Children don't give gifts or buy dinner as they do for their mother on Mother's Day. On Father's Day (a day off work), men gather together, usually outdoors and celebrate with each other, away from their families. So if you're ever in Germany and notice groups of men celebrating outside together, it might be Father's Day.

Every **New Year's Eve** since 1972, it has been a tradition for Germans to watch a particular movie called **Dinner for One.** This movie is in English and is a 1963 black-and-white short film from England. The movie is only 18 minutes long and more like a skit. Many Germans find this movie hilarious and often play it in a loop at New Year's Eve house parties. These Germans can repeat the movie's best lines if you ask them. If you're curious, you can watch Dinner for One on YouTube (it's OK for kids).

*The same procedure as last year Miss Sophie?

*most famous line from Dinner for One

Traditions in Germany

Kaffe und Kuchen (coffee and cake) is like Britain's afternoon tea, except not as dainty. In the late afternoon, Germans like to get together for a bit of catch-up with co-workers, friends or family. When they do, they like to serve coffee and cake.

Hold your applause. In Germany, it's normal to clap your hands at the theatre or a concert, but never at work or school. If Germans want to applaud a lecture or a presentation, they do it by knocking on their desk, not clapping their hands.

Concert 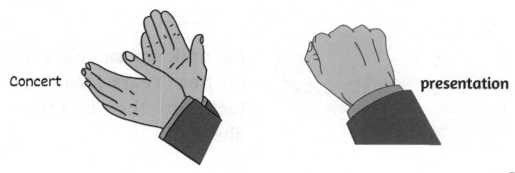 presentation

German Superstitions

Rather than cross their fingers, Germans press their thumbs for luck.

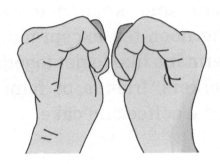

If you give your partner shoes as a gift, then it's your fault if they walk out of your life. If you give someone a knife it will cut the ties of your friendship.

To wish someone a happy birthday before the actual date is to wish them a year of bad luck. You can celebrate your birthday late, but never early.

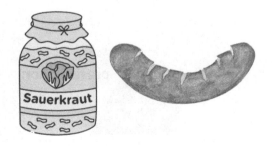

Eat pork and sauerkraut on New Years for good luck in the months ahead.

Strange German Laws

It's OK to drive naked in Germany, but it's against the law to get out of your car if you do.

It's against the law to wash your car at home - you must take it to a designated carwash.

You can not speak to a police officer informally. Remember **not** to refer to them as "du" (informal "you").

Pillows are classified as a "passive weapon" in Germany, so if you hit someone with a pillow, you can be charged with assault.

Pets in Germany

Germans love their animals. 26% of German households own a cat, and 21% own a dog.

The most popular cat names are:
- Felix
- Minka
- Moritz
- Charly
- Tiger

The most popular dog names are:
- Max
- Bruno
- Otto
- Heidi
- Emma

It's easy to own a cat in Germany because there are not a lot of rules other than to care for them properly. Cats can even roam the neighbourhood if they want, as long as the owner takes responsibility for their behaviour.

If you bring your cat, dog or ferret into Germany, you must get a pet passport. This document must include a microchip number and vaccination history.

Dog Rules in Germany

Shops, hotels, bars, and restaurants, as long as your dog is well-behaved, he is welcome pretty much everywhere in Germany (except in a grocery store).

It's good that dogs can go with you to many places because Germany has a new law regarding dogs: The law is called Hundeverordnung (Dogs Act). This law states that all dogs must be walked at least twice a day, and each walk must be at least one hour. The new rules also state that a dog can't be left alone all day, nor can they be left on a chain or a lead for long periods of time.

The Most Popular Sports in Germany

1. Football (soccer)
2. Boxing
3. Golf
4. Ice Hockey
5. Baseball
6. Motorsport
7. Tennis
8. Cycling
9. Basketball
10. Handball

The National Sort in Germany is Football

So Why is There a Picture of Soccer?

In Germany and most countries worldwide, soccer is called football. So what do they call football? They call it American Football. It all sounds very confusing. Just know that when you are in Germany, and someone asks if you want to play football, they mean soccer if you are from North America.

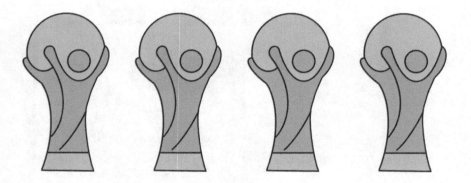

Germany has one of the best national football teams in the world. They won The World Cup in 1954, 1974, 1990 and 2014. They tied Italy for second place (Brazil won five times).

Auf Wiedersehen! (Goodbye!)

After learning so much about Germany, you can understand why it is one of the most visited countries in Europe. Germany has everything from magnificent castles to mysterious forests to modern cities. You'll get some of the most fantastic food you'll ever eat. Germany is a clean and very safe country for a family to visit.

About the Author

Collette Valliear is a world-traveller and proud G-Mom to Julien and Beau! She loves to write about travelling and is excited to help inspire others to embrace their inner vagabond. Collette has visited all seven continents and looks forward to taking her grandsons on some epic adventures one day! They love to request books and contribute new ideas often. Collette is a former property manager in Toronto, Canada, who turned her retirement into a brand new chapter of adventure and creativity!

To see more books by Meonatrip, scan the QR code below.

Please leave an honest review on Amazon; it will go a long way to creating more books like this one.

Acknowledgements:

Forward "Dusseldorf, Germany" by rick ligthelm is licensed under CC BY 2.0.

Pg 7 "Euro Denominations" by Images_of_Money is licensed under CC BY 2.0.

Pg 8 "German flag" by fdecomite is licensed under CC BY 2.0.

Pg 8 "Belgium Flag" by fdecomite is licensed under CC BY 2.0.

Pg 13 "Pattern of Houses - Esslingen Neckar - Stuttgart - Germany" by Cesar I. Martins is licensed under CC BY 2.0.

Pg 13 "Apartment buildings in Rykestrasse" by Helge Høifødt is licensed under CC BY-SA 4.0.

Pg 14 "P1185316 Tiny House" by tottr is licensed under CC BY-SA 2.0.

Pg 14 "File:2010-07-10 Berlin Flutgraben Landwehrkanal Wohnboote.jpeg" by Sir James is licensed under CC BY-SA 3.0.

Pg 20 "Berlin train station" by pnoeric is licensed under CC BY-SA 2.0.

Pg 20 "Frankfurt - ICE Train at Station" by roger4336 is licensed under CC BY-SA 2.0.

Pg 21 "Autobahn A1" by jphintze is licensed under CC BY-SA 2.0.

Pg 21 "Landing in Frankfurt - Autobahn A5" by vladislav.bezrukov is licensed under CC BY 2.0.

Pg 23 "bike park" by perke is licensed under CC BY 2.0.

Pg 26 "Brandenburg Gate - Berlin, Germany - Travel photography" by Giuseppe Milo (www.pixael.com) is licensed under CC BY 2.0.

Pg 26 "File:Remnant Section of Berlin Wall - Berlin Wall Memorial - Eastern Berlin - Germany.jpg" by Adam Jones, Ph.D. is licensed under CC BY-SA 3.0.

Pg 27 "File:Unidentified reptile - Museum fur Naturkunde, Berlin - DSC00130.JPG" by Daderot is marked with CC0 1.0.

Pg 27 "File:Berliner Zoo Bao-Bao 1.JPG" by Times is licensed under CC BY-SA 3.0.

Pg 28 "Pink Pipes" by onnola is licensed under CC BY-SA 2.0.

Pg 29 "Revaler Straße Pink Pipes (15349385156)" by Tony Webster from Portland, Oregon, United States is licensed under CC BY 2.0.

Pg 29 "Pink pipe" by ingo.ronner is licensed under CC BY 2.0.

Pg 30 "Munich: surfing in the English Garden" by *rboed* is licensed under CC BY 2.0.

Pg 30 "File:Soltau - Poststraße - Spielzeugmuseum 08 ies.jpg" by Frank Vincentz is licensed under CC BY-SA 3.0.

Pg 31 "Neuschwanstein Castle" by cjsingh is licensed under CC BY 2.0.

Acknowldegements:

Pg 32 "Alpsee-Coaster - panoramio" by qwesy qwesy is licensed under CC BY 3.0.

Pg 34 "Miniatur Wunderland, St. Michaelis" by bstrasser is licensed under CC BY-SA 2.0.

Pg 34 "File:Gothic-Cologne-Cathedral-006.jpg" by Photo-collage by User:MathKnight from photos of User:Wirginiusz Kaleta, Neuwieser, Judith Strücker, FJK71, Thomas Wolf and Max Hasak is licensed under CC BY-SA 3.0.

Pg 36 "Heidelberg Castle" by Laenulfean is licensed under CC BY-SA 2.0.

Pg 38 "Fastnacht-Umzug-Heidelberg-2011-118.jpg" by HDValentin is licensed under CC BY-SA 2.0.

Pg 38 "Fastnacht-Umzug-Heidelberg-2011-047.jpg" by HDValentin is licensed under CC BY-SA 2.0.

Pg 39 "588. Striezelmarkt Riesenschwibbbogen 2022" by VSchagow is licensed under CC BY-SA 4.0.

Pg 42 "Image" by punctuated is licensed under CC BY 2.0.

Pg 64 " Hohenzollern Castle - Stuttgart, Germany " by Trodel is licensed under CC BY-SA 2.0 .

MEONATRIP
2023

Made in the USA
Las Vegas, NV
12 November 2023

80694489R00044